GARBAGE TRUCKS

by Nancy Dickmann

PEBBLE
a capstone imprint

Pebble Emerge is published by Pebble, an imprint of Capstone.
1710 Roe Crest Drive
North Mankato, Minnesota 56003
www.capstonepub.com

Library of Congress Cataloging-in-Publication Data
Names: Dickmann, Nancy, author.
Title: Garbage trucks / by Nancy Dickmann.
Description: North Mankato : Pebble, [2022] | Series: Wild about wheels | Includes bibliographical references and index. | Audience: Ages 6-8 | Audience: Grades 2-3 | Summary: "Did you know that the average American throws away about 4.5 pounds of garbage every day? That's a lot of garbage! Garbage trucks are hard at work picking up this garbage. They carry the trash to landfills and other places. Young readers will learn about the types of garbage trucks, their main parts, and how they work"-- Provided by publisher.
Identifiers: LCCN 2020025534 (print) | LCCN 2020025535 (ebook) | ISBN 9781977132352 (hardcover) | ISBN 9781977133298 (paperback) | ISBN 9781977154293 (ebook pdf)
Subjects: LCSH: Refuse collection vehicles--Juvenile literature.
Classification: LCC TD792 .D53 2022 (print) | LCC TD792 (ebook) | DDC 628.4/420284--dc23
LC record available at https://lccn.loc.gov/2020025534
LC ebook record available at https://lccn.loc.gov/2020025535

Image Credits
Alamy: B Christopher, 7, DWD-photo, 12, Kathy deWitt, 6; Capstone Studio: Karon Dubke, 9, 17, 21 (paper); Getty Images: Blend Images/Don Mason, 8; iStockphoto: aislan13, 15, KingWu, cover, back cover, lucato, 16, Random Moments Photography, 4, Tony Baggett, 18–19, vm, 13; Juliette Peters: 21 (drawing); Shutterstock: Alf Ribeiro, 14, Mike Dotta, 11, Nattapol_Sritongcom (background), throughout, Rob Crandall, 5

Editorial Credits
Editor: Amy McDonald Maranville; Designer: Cynthia Della-Rovere; Media Researcher: Eric Gohl; Production Specialist: Katy LaVigne

All internet sites appearing in back matter were available and accurate when this book was sent to press.

Printed and bound in China.   004205

Table of Contents

Words in **bold** are in the glossary.

WHAT GARBAGE TRUCKS DO

A big truck is coming down the street. It's a garbage truck! It moves slowly. It stops in front of each house. People have put their trash cans out.

The truck picks up a trash can. The trash dumps inside the truck's **container**. The truck moves on.

Some garbage trucks collect paper or glass. Others pick up plastic or metal. Some even take yard waste. These things can be **recycled**. They can be made into new things.

There is a lot to pick up. How will it all fit? The truck has a **compactor**. It squeezes the trash. Now more will fit.

compactor

Look Inside

A garbage truck is big and tough. It has a **cab** in the front. The driver sits in the cab. The truck follows a **route**. It drives by the same houses. A map shows where to go.

Sometimes there are controls in the cab. The driver uses them. An arm can pick up trash cans. The compactor can run. The driver does not need to get out.

The truck is full. It's time to empty it! Recyclable materials can go to a recycling center. The rest often goes to a **landfill**. This is a big place where trash is dumped. Sometimes it is buried.

The back of the truck opens. There is a big blade inside. It pushes out the trash. Sometimes the container lifts up. The trash falls out.

Look Outside

Trash cans are heavy. The parts of a garbage truck are strong. Can you see the metal tubes on this truck? They are **hydraulics**. They help lift heavy things.

Sometimes controls are on the outside of a truck. A worker presses buttons. They make parts on the truck move.

A garbage truck has a **hopper**. Trash goes into it. On some trucks the hopper is at the very back. On other trucks it is just behind the cab.

This truck is a rear loader. The hopper is in the back. Sometimes rear loaders have two hoppers. There is one for trash. There is another for recycling.

Some trucks have metal arms. They lift trash cans and bins. The arms tip them into the truck. Some arms are at the front. They lift bins over the cab.

This truck is a side loader. It has an arm at the side. Up the trash can goes!

GARBAGE TRUCK DIAGRAM

cab

compactor

hopper

trash can

controls

19

Garbage Trucks in Your Neighborhood

Have you seen garbage trucks before? Do they work in your area? If a garbage truck comes to your home, watch it from your window.

What kind of garbage truck is it? Is it a rear loader? Is it a side loader? How does it pick up the trash cans? Draw the garbage truck.

If a garbage truck doesn't come to your home, make up your own!

Glossary

cab (KAB)—the compartment at the front of a truck where the driver sits

compactor (kum-PACK-tur)—a part of a garbage truck that squeezes and squashes trash

container (kun-TANE-ur)—the part at the back of a garbage truck where trash is stored

hopper (HOP-ur)—the part of a garbage truck where trash is poured before it gets squashed

hydraulics (high-DRAW-licks)—parts that use liquid to push rods in and out

landfill (LAND-fil)—a place where trash is taken by garbage trucks after people throw it away

recycled (ri-SYE-kuhld)—used again by being made into new products

route (ROUT)—the path that a garbage truck follows to reach all of its stops

Read More

Morrison, Marie. *Garbage Trucks*. New York: PowerKids Press, 2020.

Richmond, Ben. *Where Do Garbage Trucks Go?: And Other Questions About Trash and Recycling*. New York: Sterling Children's Books, 2016.

Shores, Erika L. *How Garbage Gets from Trash Cans to Landfills*. North Mankato, MN: Capstone Press, 2016.

Internet Sites

A Day in the Life of a Garbage Man
www.youtube.com/watch?v=M9jow5F_pn0

Garbage Truck Safety Tips for Kids
www.youtube.com/watch?v=aNrX4MZxszo

Where Does Garbage Go?
www.budgetdumpster.com/resources/where-does-trash-go.php

Index